GROWING INTO GENEROSITY

*God's Call
to Greater
Financial
Faithfulness*

I0098667

CLARK DICKERSON

Contents

Reading Clark Dickerson's ten principles of Christian stewardship in this book was convicting but also encouraging. Dr. Dickerson has served as our stewardship consultant for many years, and his biblically based stewardship principles turned our giving and our approach to raising support for our ministry around. This engaging and easy-to-read book is one every Christian leader needs to read. It will change the way you think about giving and the stewardship of all of life.

Dr. Matt Pinson, President, Welch College

Clark has done a truly amazing job of introducing compelling stories that draw the reader in and then follows up with powerful, scripturally based points. He has a way of introducing some deep and profound concepts in a manner that is easy to digest.

Dr. Brad Moser, President,
Clarksville Christian School

Dr. Clark Dickerson, who is my colleague, mentor, and friend, has provided a written treasure about God's economy and how his kingdom works according to three foundational principles. It is replete with redemptive vignettes concerning stewardship and anchored in solid biblical instruction. This succinct, enjoyable read is both convicting and inspiring. One cannot help but consider their role in the kingdom while reading this book. Clark is truly a legendary fundraiser. He has demonstrated good stewardship throughout his life in so many ways. And so too now by authoring this book.

Shawn Saunders, CFRE, MA, Author of *The Asker*

For nearly fifty years, Clark has taught many of us to be honest, genuine, and sincere as we do the work of stewardship development. This book is full of examples that prove his approach is classic wisdom that should be followed. Thank you, Clark—can't wait to see a second volume.

David Duncan, Principal, 1090 Strategies

I recently read Clark Dickerson's new book, *Growing into Generosity*. Having personally worked with Dickerson and Associates on two different capital campaigns, I knew that Clark's book would be biblical, clear, and relevant. It's just the way he communicates both in person and in print. Written with appeal to both leaders and laymen, this small but powerful book would be a great resource for small groups [processing the study questions at the end of each chapter] as well as personal reflection [on the action steps at the end of each chapter]. The illustrations from Clark's many years of experience in the field of resourcing Christian churches and ministries are totally relatable and engaging.

Ken Idleman, V.P. of Leadership Development, The Solomon Foundation

Foreword

In these pages Clark identifies and answers a question that has plagued pastors, Christian educators, and ministry leaders who have been challenged in their efforts to see their visions fulfilled. The question? *Why aren't Christians more generous?*

While conceding that a significant number of Christians do practice generosity, Clark uses his decades of personal experience and careful research to identify ten reasons why followers of Christ fail to exercise the generosity our Savior's grace demands. But he doesn't stop there. In each chapter, Clark provides a biblical foundation, practical and personal illustrations, and workable solutions to guide Christian leaders who want to teach and promote biblical generosity.

During my years as president of a Christian college, I had the privilege of working with Clark in capital campaign development, and I witnessed firsthand his integrity, commitment to biblical stewardship principles, and practical understanding of how to motivate those who are capable of supporting God's work. I heartily recommend *Growing into Generosity* to anyone serving in leadership in a church or faith-based school or ministry—or for that matter, anyone who wants to better understand the principles and practices of biblical generosity.

—**Don Hawkins**, DMin, president/CEO of Encouragement Communications, author of over twenty-five books, including *Never Give Up* and *Friends in Deed*

Acknowledgments

I want to thank Dr. Don Hawkins for his encouragement and guidance. Without his assistance, *Growing into Generosity* would not have been completed. I also want to thank my wife, Sherry, for her persistent encouragement over the years to "write a book."

Introduction

She Turned Her Chair Around

Let me ask you, why do you think some Christians react so negatively when the subject of money comes up? Some years ago, I was on the receiving end of such a reaction. It became the catalyst for writing this book.

American Christians are the most generous people in the world. Some give millions to charity each year, and many give generously to their churches and other charitable causes. However, many do not give at all and others who could give more choose not to do so.

My goal in the pages that follow is to illustrate reasons why I believe many Christians are not more generous. I do so from my perspective of providing fundraising counsel for hundreds of Christian organizations over the past forty years. You may agree or disagree with me, but regardless, I hope this book will stir your thinking and be of assistance as you reflect on your personal commitment to giving as a steward of God's wealth.

A few years ago, I was invited by a long-time friend, who pastored a church in California, to provide counsel for a capital campaign to fund a new church building.

Having previously visited the church, I knew many of the members, and so I recommended the campaign begin with a dinner meeting for the four couples who comprised the church leadership team, along with the pastor and his wife. The gathering took place in a team member's backyard on a pleasant late afternoon in California. The sky was bright blue, there was a hint of a breeze, and the temperature was in the high seventies. Prior to my speaking, there was a wonderful time of fellowship, including a delicious meal.

As part of my talk, I shared the story of Ananias and Sapphira found in the fifth chapter of Acts. This first-century couple sold some property, and although they withheld some of the proceeds for themselves, they assured the apostles they were giving the entire sum they had received to be used to help others in need. As you may recall, both were struck dead. But, prior to that, Peter said:

> Ananias, why has Satan filled your heart to lie to the Holy
> Spirit and keep back part of the proceeds from the field?
> Wasn't it yours while you possessed it? And after it was sold,
> wasn't it at your disposal? Why is it that you planned this
> thing in your heart? You have not lied to men but to God.
> (Acts 5:3–4)

In other words, they did not have to sell the land or give the full amount when they did sell it. As God's stewards, it was up to them to decide the best use of this gift from the Lord. In a similar way, it is up to us to make decisions regarding what to do with the portion of God's wealth he has entrusted to each of us.

After reviewing the story from God's Word, I stressed that I was not there to tell them how much to give as giving was a personal decision made between themselves and God. I continued, saying, "As leaders I would like you to be an example to the congregation by giving as generously—even sacrificially—as your circumstances allow. However, when you make your decisions, do not call it sacrificial if it is not, for the Lord knows your heart."

At that moment, a middle-aged, well-dressed woman in the group stood up, turned her chair around, then sat down with her back to me. As I finished speaking, I looked upon nine faces and one back. Apparently, I had so incensed this woman that she felt the need to show her disdain for me and for what I said by literally turning her back to me.

From knowing her and her husband personally, I think what happened was through my words the Holy Spirit pricked her heart. Her family was among the wealthiest in the congregation. Their gift to the campaign would play a major role if the financial goal was to be reached. The turning of her chair indicated to me she had no intention of providing a leadership gift.

And of course, that was her decision to make.

But why do she and many others have such a negative attitude about giving?

Statistics from several sources indicate that, on average, Christian families give about 2.5 percent of their annual incomes to charitable causes, including what they give to their churches.[1] During the Great Depression of the 1930s, the average family gave 3.3 percent of their annual income.[2]

Surprising? You might also be surprised to know non-Christians give at about the same percentage as Christians. They just give to different causes. While research methods and definitions vary regarding tithing (give 10 percent of income to charitable causes), it is interesting to note that Church Development reports only 5 percent of all churchgoers tithe and 50 percent give less than 2 percent to charity.[3] Barna Group reports that, among all Christians, 21 percent tithe.[4]

NON-CHRISTIANS GIVE AT ABOUT THE SAME PERCENTAGE AS CHRISTIANS.

Let me emphasize, I am not saying that all Christians think like the woman at the dinner or that Christians do not give. In fact, all American families—Christian and non-Christian—combined to give $374 billion to charity in 2023. There are many very generous Christians throughout the United States; however, there are many Christians who are not very generous. Research indicates that almost 40 percent give nothing to their churches. [5] Health Research estimates that if every Christian tithed, faith organizations would have an extra $139 billion each year to assist those in need and to advance the gospel message.[6]

So, I think it is worth our time to simply ask, "Why aren't Christians more generous?"

With forty years of experience counseling Christian organizations regarding fund development, I have been blessed to interact with people from all walks of life —from the very wealthy to those below the poverty line. What intrigues me is regardless of socio-economic status, the answers people give to the question "Why aren't Christians more generous?" are the same.

In this book, you will learn some answers to that question through the people I've met. Through some of these same people, you will learn how lives can be changed by accepting and acting out what God's Word teaches about generous stewardship. And if the Christian community would fully embrace these biblical attitudes and lifestyle changes, the world could be impacted by the gospel in ways we might never have imagined—all because the people of our generous God choose to follow him in faithful generosity.

Luke 6:38

Give, and it will be given to you; a good measure—pressed down, shaken together, and running over—will be poured into your lap. For with the measure you use, it will be measured back to you.

Study Questions:

1. What prompted the author to write this book, and what is the main theme of the book?
2. What is the average percentage of annual income that Christian families give to charitable causes, and how does this compare to non-Christians?
3. What is the story of Ananias and Sapphira, and what lesson can be learned from it?
4. What is the author's goal in sharing his experiences and research in this book?
5. How can the Christian community make a significant impact if it fully embraces the principles of stewardship?
6. What is the significance of the statistic that almost 40 percent of Christians give nothing to their churches?
7. How can generosity change lives and advance the gospel message?

Action Points:

1. *Reflect on your personal giving habits.* Take time to evaluate your own generosity and consider how you can increase your giving to support Christian organizations and charitable causes.

2. *Share the story of Ananias and Sapphira with others.*
   Use this story as a teaching tool to illustrate the
   importance of honesty and integrity in giving.
3. *Consider the impact of collective generosity.* Imagine
   the potential impact on the world if the Christian
   community came together to give generously and
   support those in need.

1

Learning to be generous

When I lived in Colorado, my wife and I attended a church with about 2,500 in attendance for each of its two services. One Sunday, the pastor announced he had recently learned 25 percent of church members had not given to the church in the previous twelve months.

Dropping his head, he went on to say how he didn't like to talk about stewardship or preach about money. Then as he waved his arm side to side to signify the inclusion of the entire congregation, he said, "And I do every one of you a great disservice, and it ends today."

The sad truth is this congregation is not much different from most; nor is this pastor much different than most pastors in America.

According to Nonprofits Source, 37 percent of church members and regular attendees do not contribute financially to their churches.[7] I'm not speaking of skipping a Sunday now and then. I mean they never give to their churches. Why do people who receive the blessing of Sunday services and enjoy other church related programs never give financially?

In a January 2018 article, Randy Alcorn, author of *The Treasure Principle*, wrote, "Despite the availability of excellent study materials, only 10 percent of churches have active programs to teach biblical financial and stewardship principles." Could this statistic relate to the lack of instruction and importance placed on the topic by Christian colleges? Alcorn continued in the same article, "Only 15 percent of pastors say they've been equipped by their denominations or seminary to teach financial principles."[8]

Obviously, enough Christians give to local churches or churches would not exist. But it's interesting to note that according to Lifeway Research, in the United States, about 3,000 Protestant churches opened in 2019, but 4,500, or 87 Protestant churches a week, closed their doors.[9]

A major issue with many churches today is that most Christians give to a perceived need rather than generously. In other words, if the pastor is paid, the lights are on, the building is cool in the summer and warm in the winter, why should people give more? You might think that to be an extreme statement, but not by much. How many churches fail to reach their budgeted needs each year? How many have cut back or eliminated mission programs due to lack of finances? Yes, Christians give, but the question remains, "Why aren't Christians more generous?"

2 Corinthians 9:6–7
Remember this: The person who sows sparingly will also reap sparingly, and the person who sows generously will also reap generously. Each person should do as he has decided in his heart—not reluctantly or out of necessity, for God loves a cheerful giver.

A few years ago, while speaking at a chapel service of a Christian college and seminary (obviously, many future ministers and Christian educators comprised the audience), I challenged them to begin tithing from the money they earned from their part-time jobs. The smiling faces I had looked upon only seconds before changed as their brows wrinkled and their eyes locked on me as if I just arrived from another planet.

MOST CHRISTIANS GIVE TO A PERCEIVED NEED RATHER THAN GENEROUSLY.

When I told them I was going to write a check for $100 to the college and that I wanted each of them to match my gift prior to the end of the academic year, I thought they were going to rush the platform with pitchforks and torches. Then when I explained this would only be about $3.60 a week between now and the end of the academic year (twenty-eight weeks), many rolled their eyes while others shook their heads as if they had just heard the most outlandish, laughable comment of their lives. The expressions became even more sinister when I mentioned how the amount was about the same as one large multi-topping pizza or two grande Starbucks lattes a month.

As I explained how they could begin helping new students, just as each of them had been helped through the giving of others, they shifted uneasily in their seats with sidelong glances, as if searching for any way of escape. At the end of the year, one student had given $100 to match my challenge. Not one other student gave anything toward the challenge.

Every student there was a financial aid recipient in one form or another. Why then did the idea of giving to help those who would come after them become so radical as to be ignored or even mocked?

There are approximately 2,350 verses in the Bible dealing with giving, wealth, finances, and possessions. Sixteen of the thirty-eight parables mention money. Fifteen percent of everything Jesus said referred to money—more than his teachings on heaven and hell combined.[10] Yet so few think it is important for Christian colleges to emphasize the teaching of financial stewardship to those who will serve as ministers in our churches and administrators of our Christian schools.

Many pastors and college educators fail to teach biblical stewardship when they skirt the importance of money while discussing such parables as the prodigal son. For example, they focus on the forgiving spirit of the father and gloss over the stewardship principle. After all, there would be no reason for forgiveness if not for the monetary greed of the son.

After I finished my talk, a faculty member I had known for years rushed across the auditorium to tell me how the college had added a class on financial stewardship that semester. I applauded the addition, but this college had been in existence for over eighty years! It has since closed its doors. The reason—lack of finances.

Quite a few years earlier, I had offered the same institution and another college and seminary in the same brotherhood to provide, for free, a senior seminar series on how to teach stewardship to congregations. Both presidents turned me down and both gave me the same reason: it's too controversial. And, in case you are wondering, the second college and seminary has also closed. The reason—lack of finances.

Is it any wonder Christians don't understand their role as stewards of God's wealth if pastors who should teach stewardship principles are not well trained, or perhaps don't care to know, or even fear the discussion of the topic?

Matthew 6:21
For where your treasure is, there your heart will
be also.

Some years ago, a guest speaker at our church, a lifelong friend of our pastor, began his message by explaining that when he asked about which topic he should speak on, our pastor joked and said he should talk about sexual addiction. At that point, the guest speaker paused and said, "At least he didn't ask me to talk about money." His remark produced a laugh, as was his intention. But we all knew there was a great deal of truth in what he said.

It is often said that all pastors talk about is money. We know this is not true. Most pastors rarely, if ever, speak about money outside of a capital campaign (when money is needed for a new building) or at the end of the year (when trying to meet the budget)—and even then, pastors often speak in apologetic terms. For many churches, three sermons and a pledge card in November constitute the annual teaching on stewardship.

Is this because of concern about the negative reaction teachings on stewardship might bring? Do pastors fear the mental response from the congregation like the physical reaction I received from the lady in California who turned her chair around? Think with me for a moment about the other side of the story. If pastors don't broach the subject, then church members are robbed of the joy of giving and are unlikely to be the blessing to others that God's Word encourages and calls us all to be.

Why do so many churchgoers get upset when the subject of money is raised? I believe when God's Word about money is preached, it pierces our hearts and makes us aware of how poorly we use God's wealth. People are then faced with a choice to either change their lifestyles and use money differently or get mad at the pastor. I don't know about you, but it seems a lot easier to get mad at the pastor.

Often in life we close our minds to hearing the other side of the story. Thus, we can't be taught anything that stands in conflict with our closed-minded attitude. Opening oneself to hearing something different and learning new ways to minister to others can be an enlightening experience. Considering a new approach to giving by studying and ultimately accepting what the Bible teaches about stewardship can be life-changing. But this happens only if we have a change in attitude concerning how to better steward the wealth with which the Lord has blessed us.

Matthew 6:24

No one can be a slave of two masters, since either he will hate one and love the other, or be devoted to one and despise the other. You cannot be slaves of God and of money.

Study Questions:

1. What percentage of church members had not given to the church in the past twelve months, according to the pastor's announcement?

2. Why do some who receive the blessing of Sunday services and enjoy other church-related programs never give financially?

3. What is the significance of the statistic that only 10 percent of churches have active programs to teach biblical financial and stewardship principles?

4. How does the lack of instruction and importance placed on the topic of stewardship by Christian colleges relate to the lack of generosity among Christians?

5. What is the role of pastors in teaching stewardship principles? Why is it important?

6. How does the Bible emphasize the importance of giving and stewardship? What are a few key verses that support it?

7. What is the relationship between one's treasure and their heart, according to Matthew 6:21?

Action Points:

1. *Assess your giving.* Reflect on your own giving habits and consider how you can become more generous in your support of your local church and other Christian organizations.

2. *Seek biblical teaching.* Look for churches and Christian organizations that emphasize biblical financial and stewardship principles, and find resources to deepen your understanding of these principles.

3. *Encourage pastors to teach stewardship.* If you are a church member, encourage your pastor to preach about stewardship and financial principles, and offer to support them in their efforts to teach on these important topics.

2

Understanding your role in using God's money

While providing counsel for a school in a Western state, I met a couple whose young children attended the school. The counsel was for a capital campaign to fund the construction of a completely new campus. We were meeting to discuss their financial involvement in the campaign.

Upon entering their huge home, I was immediately impressed with the polished oak floors, beautiful stonework, and impressive paintings. There was an indoor swimming pool, gymnasium, and movie theater. The images belonged in one of those magazines you breeze through while waiting for your doctor's appointment.

We had hardly sat down around a small oak table in a magnificently decorated parlor with our beautiful coffee cups in hand when the husband raised the subject of their gift to the campaign. He said, "We heard you speak the other night and, of course, we know why you are visiting us tonight. So, we discussed our gift to the campaign. Here it is."

With that, he slid a check across the table in front of me. When I looked down, I saw the check was for $6,000—their full commitment for a three-year campaign for the construction of a new campus where their children would attend school for several more years.

I looked at the check, raised my head, and said something about which I am deeply convinced, "Thank you for giving, because many people don't."

You see, over the years, I have led many capital campaigns for Christian schools, and it has been my experience that a majority of parents don't participate. That is, they give nothing. They say, "We pay tuition, so we cannot give any more." When parents tell me that, I often say, "And I get my transmission repaired." In return I usually receive a totally "huh" blank stare. I then continue to say, "You know, the transmission of my car goes out. My car gets towed to the shop, and they fix it. I then pay them for the services they have rendered me. That's what tuition is—payment for services rendered. Tuition is not a gift."

But let's return to my meeting with the parents in their beautiful home. After thanking them, I said, "As I mentioned at the meeting you attended earlier this week, I want to make sure everyone understands the three pillars of this campaign." They affirmed to me that they wanted to hear them.

I began by telling them the first pillar comes from Psalm 24:1: God is the owner of all. And since that verse is true, and since "all" is a fully inclusive word, it means we own absolutely nothing. Nothing belongs to us. Everything we possess belongs to God.

At this point, the wife dropped her head as a sad look covered her face. The husband leaned toward me and in all sincerity said, "Even this house?" I said, "Yes, your real estate agent may tell you that you own this house, but this house is part of the 'all' that God owns." His only response to this was, "Wow!"

I then told them that pillar number two is illustrated by the story of the talents in Matthew 25:14–30, where the master of the house gave each steward money to increase on behalf of the master.

Since we don't own anything, we are stewards of God's possessions. So as stewards, as illustrated by the story of the talents, we are to make decisions that benefit the Master, not the steward. As stewards, we make decisions every day on how to spend God's money. Consequently, whether we buy a house or a hamburger, we are spend-

SINCE WE DON'T OWN ANYTHING, WE ARE STEWARDS OF GOD'S POSSESSIONS.

ing God's money. In fact, every time we spend any money at all, we are making a stewardship decision.

At this point, the husband responded hesitantly, "So you are really saying we don't own this house?"

I responded, "In the secular world you are perceived as owners, but in regard to your relationship with God, you are only stewards. Both you and I own absolutely nothing. Even if this house passes to one of your children, one day this house will be occupied by strangers. You are the stewards as long as you live here."

I noticed a tear running down the wife's cheek.

Then I explained the third pillar of the stewardship campaign is that as Christians, we are blessed so we can bless others. This is taught in Galatians 6:10: "Therefore, as we have opportunity, we must work for the good of all, especially for those who belong to the household of faith."

I explained the campaign was about blessing the children currently at the school, the children who would attend the school in the future, and beyond that, every person with whom the students would come in contact for the next ten, twenty, thirty years and beyond. Attending the school would make a difference in the lives of the students, and they in turn through their contact with others could have a role in changing others' lives for the better. I said, "Your campaign gift now will impact people for Christ whom you will never know this side of heaven. Truly, the campaign is not about constructing a new campus but rather about impacting lives for Christ."

The husband said, "I have never heard any of that before in my life." And his wife was quick to nod her agreement.

They attended church as a family for over two decades yet could not recall these simple stewardship truths ever being taught. I'd like to believe the message from these three pillars had been mentioned by their pastor at some point. But if so, obviously never in such a way for them to have had any impact on the couple's thinking regarding giving.

Next, I assured them that there is nothing wrong with Christians having nice things. Then I said, "But we need to stop and consider when enough is enough. When do we cross the line beyond taking care of our families to using too much of God's money on ourselves, as opposed to being a blessing to others?"

Continuing, I told them, "I heard you say you discussed your gift, but I didn't hear you say you had prayed about it." I asked, "Do you pray about your giving?"

They answered in unison, "No."

I told them they were in the majority, as most Christians don't pray about giving but rather budget their giving. Now there is nothing wrong with budgeting giving, but I think the reason most Christians don't pray about giving is that we are absolutely terrified of what God's answer might be.

I suggested they take some time to ask God what he would have them do in regard to the school's campaign. Then I said, "Personally, I would like you to make the lead commitment in the parents' portion of the campaign—a commitment of $250,000 over a three-year period."

Upon hearing this, the husband leaned back in his chair with arms in the air and, almost gasping, responded that such a gift was not something they had ever considered.

I said, "I understand that and, really, what I ask you to give is not important. What is important is what you believe the Lord is leading you to give."

I explained, "The Lord will lead in the area of giving if you will ask for his leadership." I urged them to take time over the next two days to specifically pray about their commitment to the campaign.

Then I added, "If you believe the Lord is giving you a gift number, that is the number. But, if after time in prayer, you don't believe you have received such a message, then do as you wish."

They agreed that they would take some time to pray about a campaign commitment, and we agreed that I would contact them in three days.

I left their $6,000 check on the table.

They beat me to the punch. The second day after my visit, they gave a check designated for the campaign for

$150,000 and made an additional three-year campaign commitment of $500,000.

They went from a one-time gift of $6,000 to $650,000 in gifts and commitments simply because someone took the time to explain their role in relationship to God and his money.

Now, I'm not saying all wealthy Christians do not give generously or that those who do not give generously will respond as this couple did.

However, if all Christians understood and embraced these simple pillars of truth about stewardship, the giving in America would increase significantly—and not just among those who are perceived to be wealthy. God's message in the Bible about stewardship is a message for all regardless of our socioeconomic status.

It's interesting how sometimes we can hear something we know applies to others and never recognize that the message also applies to us. We often see the splinters in the eyes of others while not accepting the wooden beams in our own eyes. Many people give the same amount week after week for years. They never think about inflation, nor consider what the Lord would have them do with the blessings he has provided. The Bible gives clear instructions about giving—it is the number one source for understanding one's relationship with God and his money.

Psalm 24:1

*The earth and everything in it, the world and
its inhabitants, belong to the LORD.*

Study Questions:

1. What is the main idea of the chapter, and how does it relate to the title, "Understanding your role in using God's money"?
2. How does the author's meeting with the couple illustrate the concept of stewardship?
3. What are the three pillars of the stewardship campaign mentioned in the chapter?
4. How does the author respond to the couple's initial hesitation to give more, and what is the outcome of their conversation?
5. What is the significance of the couple's decision to pray about their commitment to the campaign, and how did them doing so relate to their eventual gift?
6. How does the author address the common excuse that "we pay tuition, so we cannot give any more"?
7. What is the author's main point about the Bible's instructions on giving, and how does it relate to the chapter's theme?

Action Points:

1. *Reflect on your own relationship with God and his money.* Take time to consider how you view your possessions and finances in light of Psalm 24:1. Do

you see yourself as a steward of God's resources, or do you think of them as solely your own?

2. *Pray about your giving.* Like the couple in the chapter, take time to pray about your commitment to giving, especially in the context of capital campaigns or other initiatives that align with your values.

3. *Consider the impact of your giving.* Think about how your giving can have a ripple effect on others, both now and in the future. How can you use your resources to bless others and further God's kingdom?

3

Are you praying
about being generous?

For several years prior to the fall of the Iron Curtain, I served as the vice president of an organization that ministered in Eastern Europe. On one of my trips, I was scheduled to visit the city of Kiev (now Kyiv) in Ukraine and then continue on to Moscow.

At age eighteen, Sofia became the leader of a youth group in Kiev. About five feet, five inches with short-cropped brunette hair with bangs, a broad smile, and bright, welcoming eyes, she undertook a very dangerous role in what was then a part of the communist Soviet Union.

The purpose of my trip was to deliver Christian literature that Sofia and other teenagers would distribute on the streets of Kiev to young people to introduce them to the Lord.

As was common in those days under the communist system, a situation arose that made it impossible for me to make the trip to Kiev. Since it would not have been wise for me to attempt contact under such circumstances, I sadly passed on the trip to Kiev and traveled on to Moscow—keeping Sofia's literature in my possession.

As the mid-week evening service in Moscow was about to begin, an elder approached and told me that a young lady was at the front door asking for me. I could not imagine who this person might be, but to my surprise there stood Sofia. When I asked her how she knew I would be in Moscow—at that church, on that night, at that time—she beamed her biggest smile and said, "I didn't, but I prayed a lot. I prayed a lot."

Think about it. A teenage girl prays a lot, then trusts God's leading to travel hundreds of miles by train in hopes of securing Christian literature, which, at great personal risk, she intended to give away to total strangers. She sought God in prayer, opened herself up to his leading, and then took a step of faith based on that prayer relationship.

When it comes to financial stewardship, frequent and fervent prayer should be the fundamental ingredient. Yet often the power of prayer, while utilized by Christians in other situations, is absent when it comes to the management of God's resources.

1 Thessalonians 5:17–18
Pray constantly. Give thanks in everything, for this is
God's will for you in Christ Jesus.

Some years ago, I was blessed to provide counsel for a campaign to construct a new church building for a Midwestern congregation. Shortly after the campaign, I received a phone call from a senior couple who attended the church. They wanted to share with me how they determined the size of their campaign commitment. I never ask for such personal information and was a bit reluctant to hear them out. However, they were giggling with anticipation to tell me, so I agreed to hear their story.

They began by saying that since they didn't watch much cable TV, they decided to drop their subscription. They liked to read magazines, but they decided to cut their magazine subscriptions from twenty-six to thirteen (no, that is not a misprint). They ate out a lot, so they opted to reduce restaurant expenditures. Altogether, the estimated savings were about $3,000 a year. They multiplied that by the three years of the campaign to arrive at $9,000.

I said, "Thanks for sharing with me. I appreciate the thought you put into your commitment." They said, "Oh no, that's not our commitment."

They continued, saying that when they completed all the math, they both saw how they weren't paying heed to what they learned as part of the church stewardship campaign. They rehearsed back to me a lot of the information I had shared as the counsel for the campaign, including an often-used statement by consultants in stewardship campaigns: "not equal gifts, but equal sacrifice."

They spent time in prayer, asking the Lord's guidance about their campaign commitment. After praying, they told me they had come to the realization that they had not made a sacrificial commitment. Then they told me something which touched me greatly and has stayed with me over the years. They said, "We realized by giving up cable TV, reducing magazine subscriptions, and eating out less, we had decided to give the Lord the scraps off our life's table that we didn't want anymore."

They realized they were giving the Lord things they did not need and could not care less about. They went on to review the whole concept of sacrificial giving and prayed earnestly for guidance. Ultimately, they felt led to make a much larger commitment. They included the aforementioned life changes as part of their revised commitment of $30,000.

Had they done something incorrect by looking for ways to give to the campaign? Absolutely not! But they realized they were not truly seeking guidance in their giving or being generous givers. Rather, they had determined their giving by calculating what they could do without, instead of determining what they felt led to give and then seeking guidance as to how to reach that goal.

It has been said that Christians pray about everything in the world but money, except when they need some. Imagine the impact on the world if all Christians were to begin each day with the simple prayer "Lord, today help me to be the best steward of your wealth I can be."

Prayer is the means through which God can direct his message to you concerning your investment of his wealth. Prayer is the pathway through which God shows people how they can give far more than they otherwise would have thought.

"LORD, HELP ME BE THE BEST STEWARD OF YOUR WEALTH I CAN BE."

Frankly, we have not failed to be good stewards because we lack guidance. We have God's Word and the Lord himself. But, just like being lost on an unknown road, if we don't Google directions, open a road map, or ask for assistance, we remain lost.

You see, it is not only your giving that God has dominion over. If you have trusted the Lord as Savior and have invited him into your life, prayer is the pathway through which he will direct all areas, including your finances.

I encourage people to pray, seeking God's guidance about all things financial—including gifts to their church, a ministry campaign, or the purchase of a house or car. Sincerely opening ourselves up to God's leading is the key.

When we take the small and large personal issues to the Lord in prayer, truly seeking his direction, we begin to understand that he really does provide the way we should go—even with money.

Romans 12:12

Rejoice in hope; be patient in affliction; be persistent in prayer.

Study Questions:

1. What is the main idea of Chapter 3? How does it relate to the title, "Are you praying about being generous"?
2. What is the story of Sofia, and what does it illustrate about the power of prayer?
3. How do Christians often approach giving, and what is the problem with this approach?
4. What is the concept of "equal sacrifice" in giving? How does it relate to the story of the senior couple?
5. What is the significance of prayer in determining one's giving, and how can it impact one's generosity?
6. What is the author's encouragement to readers regarding prayer and financial decisions?
7. How does Romans 12:12 relate to the theme of prayer and giving in this chapter?

Action Points:

1. *Make prayer a priority in your giving.* Take time to pray about your financial decisions, including gifts to your church or other ministries. Ask God for guidance and direction.
2. *Seek to give generously.* Reflect on your giving habits and consider whether you are giving generously or

only giving what you don't need. Pray for guidance on how to give more generously.

3. *Start each day with a prayer of stewardship.* Begin each day with a simple prayer, such as "Lord, help me today to be the best steward of your wealth I can be." This can help you cultivate a mindset of stewardship and generosity.

4

Do you control your possessions (or do they control you)?

The story is told about Minnesota Fats, a famous pool player of days gone by. He was scheduled to compete in a pool tournament in Detroit. After arriving a day early, he decided to visit a neighborhood pool hall and play with some of the locals just for fun. A young man watched in amazement as the legendary Fats lost a game of eight-ball.

The young man sidled up to Fats and said in an almost reverent tone, "What's the deal? I thought you never lost." As the story goes, Fats placed his hand on the green felt of the pool table and replied, "Son, I never lose when money is on the table."

While perhaps a bit humorous, the story makes a crucial point. When *money* is involved, everything changes. A major cause of divorce, dissolving of partnerships, severing of long-standing friendships, and other personal heartbreaks is money and the disputes it causes between people.

When it comes to money and the things money buys, people can easily lose perspective. Indeed, it is not unusual for people to reach a point where they do not own their possessions, but their possessions own them.

Unfortunately, Christians are not immune to this condition.

Luke 12:16–21

A rich man's land was very productive. He thought to himself, "What should I do, since I don't have anywhere to store my crops? I will do this," he said. "I'll tear down my barns and build bigger ones and store my grain and my goods there. Then I'll say to myself, 'You have many goods stored up for many years. Take it easy; eat, drink, and enjoy yourself.'" But God said to him, "You fool! This very night your life is demanded of you. And the things you have prepared—whose will they be?" That's how it is with the one who stores up treasure for himself and is not rich toward God.

Between the two worship services of a large suburban church, I taught a forty-five-minute lesson to about three hundred and fifty people on financial management. I didn't have the time to deal with the topic in-depth, so I focused on the three stewardship pillars:

- God is the owner of all   Psalm 24:1
- We are stewards, not owners   Matthew 25:14–30
- We are blessed to bless others   Galatians 6:10

I was supposed to meet with the pastor in his office for prayer prior to the second service. He never made it to his office but joined me on the platform at the start of the service. He whispered in my ear, "I'll tell you later." Following the service, he explained to me what had happened.

He asked me if I remembered a particular couple from the financial management session. Even though it was a large group, the couple did stand out. They arrived just as I was beginning and walked along the back of the room to find seats. She was about six feet tall, had long blonde hair, and wore a stylish bright red pantsuit accented with beautiful jewelry. He was about six feet, three inches tall, with a dark complexion and slicked back jet-black hair, and he wore a tailored dark blue suit.

They had met the pastor in the hallway and asked to speak with him. Knowing I would be in his office, he directed them to an empty classroom. As the door closed, they both began to cry. She apologized for not being at church for several months. He explained it was because they were not living together. She was currently living in the house that they were about to lose due to foreclosure—in addition to the other two in other states that they had already lost. Home for him was a local, extended-stay hotel. They had no children.

It turned out that he had lost his job with an annual income of over $600,000. While the severance package was significant, it was eventually spent, and they were soon to be without funds. They explained how the only things they truly owned were the clothes in their closets and some of their jewelry. Everything else—house, cars, boat, RV, you name it—had been purchased using credit.

Their cash had been spent on luxurious vacations, expensive dining out, gifts to relatives, and the like. And now, even their high-level credit cards were about to be maxed out. They had no savings, no stocks—nothing they could cash in that would have any significant impact on their desperate financial situation. They explained that the tension over their financial straits had caused them to blame one another for overspending, for not planning, for failing to save, and for losing their source of income.

She explained how she had seen in the church newsletter that a man was going to speak on financial management. She had talked her husband into attending, and they drove their soon-to-be repossessed luxury cars to the church, met in the parking lot, and walked in together.

They asked the pastor if what that guy had said was true. When assured it was true, they said they had never heard such teaching before and didn't understand how something from the Bible could possibly help manage finances in today's world. However, hearing those simple three pillars with illustrations from other people's lives had caused them to realize how they had allowed themselves to get caught in the trap of money and possessions—to the point that they did not own their possessions but their possessions owned them.

That day they resolved to make a change. They reunited. Both secured jobs, though the combined income was much less than what the husband had been making on his own. They did lose their huge home, fancy cars, and most of their possessions which had previously seemed so important.

In the process, though, they discovered a caring God who wants only the best for his children and learned the things money can buy are not all that important. They saw how importance lies in the good God's wealth can bring to this world. They asked God to forgive them for, in their words, "squandering God's provision." They developed a budget on which to live, began donating to their church and other charities, and spoke to their pastor of the joy they received by, in some small way, being a blessing to others in need.

Later the pastor shared with me that during one of their counseling sessions, they had reflected on the wealth that had once possessed them. They spoke of their biggest regret being that they had done nothing to help others with God's money. The sad thing for them was that no matter what they did with money in the future, they would never be able to use the money they had squandered for the good which God had intended it.

They felt remorseful of being poor stewards of God's wealth. You see, they had been in the 37 percent category—despite having stewardship over millions of dollars, they never gave a dime to their church or any charitable cause.

Proverbs 11:24, 28
One person gives freely, yet gains more; another with-holds what is right, only to become poor. . . . Anyone trusting in his riches will fall, but the righteous will flourish like foliage.

DESPITE HAVING STEWARDSHIP OVER MILLIONS OF DOLLARS, THEY NEVER GAVE A DIME.

One of my favorite TV commercials involves a heavy metal concert, a teenage guy, and a broken guitar. I'm sure those paying for the commercial would be disappointed to know I have forgotten what they were selling, but the storyline made an impression on me regarding our relationship to God and his money.

In the commercial, the concert ends and a member of the band smashes his guitar on the stage and flings it into the crowd. An absolute frenzy follows as all the young concert-goers fight over the guitar. People push and shove and crawl on the floor, trying to get their hands on the broken guitar.

One teenage boy manages to secure it and runs from the crowd. Several in the crowd chase after him—or more accurately, they chase after the smashed guitar. They continue to pursue him as he exits the arena and runs down the street. The young man ducks down an alley and into a darkened doorway. Not seeing him in the doorway, the mob rushes past him.

The young man steps out from the darkness and begins walking down the dirty, garbage-strewn alley, away from those who were chasing him. He comes upon an open dumpster. He looks at the dumpster, looks at the broken guitar, tosses the guitar into the dumpster, and walks away.

The prized possession that he, and many others, had thought was so very important was easily discarded only minutes after he obtained it. While we may not attend a rock concert and may not chase after a useless guitar, we often pursue things we think are important—phones, cars, larger homes, nicer clothes, and on and on. And, once we possess them, with the excitement of the chase gone, we take them for granted or discard them to chase after the next broken guitar.

Many homes are cluttered with items impulsively purchased and then laid aside—put in a closet, basement, or storage unit five miles from our homes—and stay there until we move. Then they find their place in a new closet, basement, or storage unit five miles from our new homes.

The world would be quite different if we took our stewardship role seriously and began using God's money to bless others instead of allowing our possessions to own us.

Luke 12:15

Watch out and be on guard against all greed because one's life is not in the abundance of his possessions.

Do you control your possessions (or do they control you)?

Study Questions:

1. What is the main idea of Chapter 4, and how does it relate to the concept of generosity?
2. What is the story of Minnesota Fats, and what point does it illustrate about money and possessions?
3. How do Christians often view their possessions? What is the problem with this perspective?
4. How do the three stewardship pillars relate to the story of the couple who lost their wealth?
5. How did the couple's perspective on money and possessions change after hearing the teaching on financial management?
6. What is the significance of Proverbs 11:24, 28 in relation to the concept of generosity and possessions?
7. What is the author's main point about the pursuit of wealth and possessions? How does it relate to Luke 12:15?

Action Points:

1. *Reflect on your relationship with possessions.* Take time to consider how you view your possessions and wealth. Do you see them as a blessing to be used for God's purposes, or do you tend to prioritize accumulating more?

2. *Evaluate your priorities.* Ask yourself whether your priorities align with God's values. Are you using your resources to bless others, or are you primarily focused on accumulating wealth and possessions?

3. *Consider a change in perspective.* Reflect on the story of the couple who lost their wealth and how their perspective changed. Ask God to help you see your possessions and wealth from a biblical perspective and consider how you can use what you have been given to bless others.

5

Accept the challenge to be generous

The board of directors of a Christian school asked me to come to their assistance. They were attempting a capital campaign to construct new facilities and were woefully short of the monetary goal.

It is quite challenging to "redo" a campaign when there is public knowledge of a "failed" effort in the immediate past. But, after meeting with the leadership, seeing the school's operation, and reviewing the constituency, it became clear to me that none of those things was the problem. The reason for the disappointing results was how the campaign had been conducted.

I suggested they begin again as if nothing had been done—even to the point of reengaging the board of directors who had already made commitments to the previous campaign effort. To begin the process, a campaign kick-off meeting was planned for the board members and their spouses.

The chair of the board and his wife, parents of students at the school, were very positive about the campaign and agreed to host the meeting. They had a spacious home impeccably decorated throughout. They paid for a local caterer to provide the desserts to be served that evening.

The school's director of development agreed to follow up with the board members to ask for their financial commitments. However, the head of school asked if I would meet with the chair and his wife. Due to the gentleman's extremely busy business travel schedule for the following two weeks, the only opportunity for us to meet was thirty minutes before the start of the meeting with the board members and spouses. I felt confident that, due to their extremely positive attitude and the portion of God's wealth they oversaw as stewards, the meeting would go well.

I could not have been more wrong.

To begin with, because the meeting was taking place in their home with people mingling about, the only place we could meet to ensure privacy was in their bedroom. There was only one chair in the room, so I sat in the chair and they sat on the end of the bed. Certainly not the best of situations, but we all three laughed at the arrangement. Again, I thought the meeting would go well.

I reminded them of the biblical stewardship pillars serving as the foundation of the campaign, reviewed the campaign mission, stressed the importance of leadership giving, and asked them to give $50,000 over the next three years.

Their response was immediate—and not good.

They acted offended and the gentleman said, "Who do you think you are to ask us for such a gift?" I could see in his wife's face that she was thinking the same thing. They stated—in as heated a voice as the circumstance of others just outside the bedroom door would permit—several reasons why such a gift was not possible. As they continued their tirade, another board member knocked on the door and announced it was time to start the meeting. I quickly left the room.

The meeting with the entire board and spouses went well. However, I was very perplexed as I listened to the Chairman speak passionately about the need to financially support the campaign. I spoke after him and told those gathered basically the same thing I had shared with the Chairman and his wife. I explained that the director of development would contact each family within the next few days to set up appointments to visit with them about their commitments.

Due to my 6 a.m. flight and a long drive to the hotel next to the airport, I needed to leave shortly after the meeting adjourned. Prior to leaving, I said my goodbyes with handshakes and best wishes to every family. However, as I approached the Chairman and his wife, they turned their backs and walked away. It's the only time in my life that my extended hand was left untouched.

As I drove the forty-five minutes to the Comfort Inn with the rain falling on the windshield, I rehearsed our meeting in my mind. I knew the environment had not been the best, but that alone could not account for the almost out-of-control negative response.

As my head hit the pillow, I felt at peace that I had done nothing more than present the case for support and asked them to give in accordance with what they could do if they so desired. I closed my eyes for what was to be a short night's rest.

Around 11 p.m. I was awakened by a knock on the door. I looked through the peephole, and there stood the Chairman of the board. He is a big man, over six feet on a 250-pound frame, but somehow, he looked less domineering standing there sopping wet. Obviously, he had forgotten an umbrella, as the rain had increased to a major storm with crackling lightning and loud thunder.

I asked if his wife was with him as I was in my pajamas. Finding out she was not present and after checking his hands for weapons, I opened the door, invited him in, and offered him a towel. He had a big grin on his face, and before any words were exchanged, he gave me a huge bear hug. Then, he joyously told me they were going to give the $50,000. He was almost giddy with excitement. It reminded me of Scrooge after awakening from his sleep on Christmas Day.

Of course I was very pleased, but also very confused. I said, "That's wonderful, but what changed your mind?"

He told me he and his wife were so mad at me they knew they couldn't go to sleep, so they drove around their neighborhood—even though the meeting had been in their home—in the rain talking about what had happened.

He told me that for several minutes, they exchanged criticisms of me, even more blunt than those they had spoken to me. I couldn't imagine any worse comments but didn't say anything. He continued, saying that after several minutes, they began to discuss the campaign, their role as leaders, and the good that would be accomplished should the campaign be successful—not only for the current students but also for future students and for the community at large.

He went on to say that after a short time of silence, his wife looked at him and said, "What is it Clark always says? God is the owner of all. We are stewards, not owners. We are blessed to bless others. Of course we can give the $50,000." He wanted to tell me in person, so he drove forty-five minutes in a rainstorm to do so.

You see, it wasn't the $50,000. In retrospect, they could have given even more. The problem was that no one had ever challenged them to give such a gift. They were accustomed to the weekly offering at church where they wrote the same check week after week after week. During our late night/early morning discussion, he told me they didn't tithe at church and didn't give to anything else except the school's jog-a-thon each year. However, he also told me how they were going to change because, for the first time in their lives, they were challenged to give. And, through that challenge, they came to the realization that they needed to be conscientious stewards of God's wealth in order to bless God's people.

THEY NEEDED TO BE CONSCIENTIOUS STEWARDS OF GOD'S WEALTH TO BLESS GOD'S PEOPLE.

Through my interactions with people over the years, I have seen that when people rise to meet a financial challenge, they often realize that is where they should have been all along. They find great joy in understanding that the Lord has blessed them so they can be a blessing to others.

1 Timothy 6:17–19

Instruct those who are rich in the present age not to be arrogant or to set their hope on the uncertainty of wealth, but on God, who richly provides us with all things to enjoy. Instruct them to do what is good, to be rich in good works, to be generous, willing to share, storing up for themselves a good reserve for the age to come, so that they may take hold of life that is real.

Study Questions:

1. What was the initial reaction of the Chairman and his wife to the request for a $50,000 donation, and what did their reaction reveal about their perspective on giving?

2. How did their attitude toward giving change after their conversation following the meeting, and what triggered the change?

3. How do the three stewardship principles relate to the story of the Chairman and his wife?

4. What is the author's main point about challenging people to give? How does it relate to the story of the Chairman and his wife?

5. How does the author's experience with the Chairman and his wife illustrate the importance of taking time to evaluate how we use the Lord's money?

6. What does 1 Timothy 6:17–19 teach about the responsibilities of those who are wealthy? How does it relate to the story of the Chairman and his wife?

7. What is the significance of the Chairman's statement that they were going to change? What did it reveal about their newfound understanding of stewardship?

Action Points:

1. *Reflect on your own giving habits.* Ask God to help you develop a heart of generosity and challenge yourself when giving opportunities are made known.
2. *Challenge others to give.* Consider how you can encourage others to give generously, whether through a fundraising campaign or simply by sharing your own experiences of generosity.
3. *Seek giving opportunities.* Be on the alert for giving opportunities in your community.

6

Giving is part of your service to God

The elders of a large suburban church, with an upper-middle-class congregation, invited me to review their program to help determine why they were consistently short in meeting their budgeted obligations. They complained of the congregation's lack of vision and described them as very tight regarding money.

I studied their attendance and financial records. I interviewed the pastor and other leaders about how they went about determining the church budget. I reviewed what was cut from the budget in recent years when the desired gifting level was not reached.

As a result of my research, I realized the leadership looked at weekly giving more like income, like how a business would view money received for selling a product. It was probably not a conscious thought, and I didn't think they would ever admit to viewing giving in that way. But it was obvious they saw weekly offerings as a means of having money to pay bills.

You can imagine my anticipation when, as part of my review, I attended a worship service. (Only the church leadership team knew I was anyone but a casual visitor.) I tried to observe as much as I could about the congregation.

I looked around the parking lot prior to entering the church and observed people as they gathered for the morning service. It appeared the vast majority in attendance, at least on the surface, had sufficient funds to afford some of life's better stuff. I was warmly greeted as I entered, encouraged to have coffee and a doughnut, and invited back as I left. One couple even invited me to lunch.

During the service, the music, the announcements, the communion, and the sermon were all presented in a professional manner that well fit the personality of the congregation.

Six minutes from the scheduled time for the close of the service, I realized not a word had been spoken about giving or an offering. After the extremely professional worship team led the congregation in singing a hymn, one of the singers stepped forward and simply announced, "We will now take the offering."

She stepped back into the group of five as if the movement was choreographed. They sang a wonderfully arranged song, as professionally as you would hear at a Christian concert, while ushers hurriedly passed offering bags—the kind you can put your hand into without anyone knowing whether you gave or not. As the voices faded and the song came to an end, the same woman stepped forward and said, "Thank you for coming. We are dismissed."

Every part of the service—sermon, communion, and music—had been presented as ministry. But, when the opportunity came for the congregation to make stewardship decisions and invest a portion of God's wealth, it was as if the church leadership was embarrassed to ask people to participate.

During the service, nothing was mentioned about giving. God's Word was not opened regarding giving, there was no prayer over the offering, and very little time was taken in the offering collection. Investing God's wealth was not looked upon as ministry but rather as a means to meet a budget.

In my report to the church leadership, I asked them to begin a stewardship teaching program using Sunday School lessons and sermons I provided and to make the offering time an integral part of the worship service. I also invited them to initiate a 1 percent program. A 1 percent program encourages all families in the church to give 1 percent more of their income than what they currently give.

As I thought would be the case, most families had no idea what percentage they gave. To determine what a 1 percent increase would be, the program forced most in the congregation to come to grips with the reality that on a percentage basis, they gave very little. I learned later that the combination of the stewardship emphasis and the 1 percent program led many in the congregation to give double or triple what they had been giving to the church. The program was the impetus for a total revamping of how the pastor and other church leaders presented giving and the role of stewardship to the congregation. The new emphasis on teaching stewardship not only resulted in budget increases for new programs but also taught individual members to seek giving opportunities to reach others for the kingdom.

Exodus 35:21

Everyone whose heart was moved and whose spirit prompted him came and brought an offering to the Lord for the work on the tent of meeting, for all its services, and for the holy garments.

In December 1981, while ministering in communist Eastern Europe, I visited Poland. It was a trip that changed my perception of stewardship. I was leading a group that provided several tightly packed semi-trailers full of needed food, clothing, personal products, and medicine to the economically devastated country. The situation was so bad that the communist government officials, contrary to their normal way of doing things, were encouraging outsiders to bring needed supplies, and there were no border inspections of the trailers.

However, the day after our arrival in Warsaw, the communist government declared martial law in response to the Solidarity movement, which focused on workers' rights and social change.

Martial law meant closed borders, a strict curfew, gasoline rationing, and soldiers stationed on every street corner. The circumstances made life for the Polish people even more difficult.

Knowing the extreme need for the items we brought, the soldiers looked the other way. This allowed us to follow our initial plan for distribution. Once the plan was implemented, something extraordinary happened.

We gave the commodities to the Christians, who had little food or other essentials. They filled baskets, buckets, and bags and then went door-to-door giving the vast majority of the necessities we had brought for them to other neighborhood families.

Why did they do that?

When I inquired of the church leaders, they smiled and said that by giving the food and supplies to others, they were practicing what the Lord spoke of regarding helping our neighbors. They hoped this action would encourage recipients to have a deeper understanding of the Lord and take that first step toward a relationship with him.

One pastor said to me, "Brother Clark, if you could give up something temporary in nature to help someone take the first step toward a permanent relationship with the Lord, wouldn't you do that?" The answer I was supposed to give was obvious. But if my family were in such dire straits, I'm not sure I—or very many other American Christians— would think the way the Polish Christians did that day.

Yes, American Christians give money to churches and other worthy causes—the commodities we were able to share resulted from gifts provided by Americans. But, giving is relative. The Polish Christians gave virtually all the food-stuffs and other products as a true expression of outreach ministry to others—to the point of true sacrifice for their own families.

The concept that we are stewards of God's wealth, and therefore make investment decisions to honor the Father, is very foreign to many American Christians. When you consider that only 10 percent of churches across denominational lines have classes or programs that teach stewardship and 37 percent or more of Christians who attend church on a regular basis never put anything in the offering plate, *it becomes easier to understand why*

WE'RE STEWARDS OF GOD'S WEALTH AND MAKE INVESTMENT DECISIONS TO HONOR THE FATHER.

many Christians do not consider giving as an integral part of their relationship with Christ.

Hebrews 13:16

Don't neglect to do what is good and to share,
for God is pleased with such sacrifices.

Study Questions:

1. What was the author's observation about the church's attitude toward giving, and how did such an attitude impact their financial situation?
2. How did the church leadership view giving, and how did it differ from the author's perspective?
3. What changes did the author recommend to the church leadership to improve their stewardship and giving practices?
4. What was the outcome of the church's new stewardship emphasis and 1 percent program? What did it reveal about the congregation's giving habits?
5. What was the attitude of the Polish Christians toward giving and stewardship? What can we learn from their example?
6. What does Exodus 35:21 teach about the motivation for giving, and how can we apply this principle in our own lives?
7. What does Hebrews 13:16 emphasize about the importance of giving and sharing with others? How can we prioritize the heart of this verse in our own lives?

Action Points:

1. *Evaluate your own giving habits.* Consider whether you view giving as an integral part of your relationship with Christ. Ask God to help you develop a heart of generosity and a willingness to sacrifice for the sake of others.
2. *Encourage your church to prioritize stewardship.* If you are involved in church leadership, consider implementing a stewardship teaching program and placing an emphasis on giving as an act of worship. If you are a church member, encourage your leaders to prioritize stewardship and generosity.
3. *Look for opportunities to give generously.* Consider how you can give beyond your regular tithe or offerings, whether through volunteering, donating to a specific cause, or simply being willing to help those in need.

7

Give when the opportunity arises

Many people think of giving only in light of the what-ifs of life . . . what if I give and my son's tuition goes up? . . . what if I give and we have another recession? . . . what if I give and . . .

You likely will never find the right time to give if you focus only on the potential negative financial events that can occur.

I'm all for people having a safety net or emergency fund, but once that's established, there should be no reason for not giving. Of course, if such a safety net is never established, the lack of it can become the ever-present negative that prevents giving. Too often, the what-ifs of our personal future keep us from giving as we know we should. And we rationalize it as necessary for our long-term goals in life—thus, it never seems to be the right time to give.

On many occasions during my forty-eight years in fund development, people have told me, "I don't want to give now because the stock market is down." Many others have told me, "I don't want to give now because the stock market is up."

THE WHAT-IFS OF OUR FUTURE KEEP US FROM GIVING AS WE SHOULD.

Sound contradictory?

The first group is saying that when the stocks come back to what they used to be, then they'll give. Of course, by the time that happens, if it happens, the campaign or special program could be over, and thus they have escaped giving.

The second group is saying the stocks are going up and "If I wait, the organization will get more for the same number of stock shares." But when does the waiting stop? By the time it reaches that magic number, the market could start going down or the campaign could be over, and thus they too have escaped giving.

I remember the story of one such donor several years ago. I was blessed to be providing capital campaign counsel for a Christian school. The school was growing significantly in numbers and programs, but like a lot of schools, they had no financial reserves and no real plan to acquire the funding for the much-needed additional facilities.

Another consultant and I worked with them to initiate a campaign with the goal of providing the necessary funding.

One friend of the school agreed to provide ten thousand shares of a particular stock, which at the time was trading for $30 per share. Obviously, that would have been a gift of $300,000—just what was needed to give the campaign a jump start and serve as an example to other major donor prospects.

However, when the gentleman was asked to transfer the stock to the school so it could be sold, his reply was, "I want to wait because the stock is increasing in value, and the ten thousand shares will be worth even more to the school."

We explained that while we appreciated his thinking, the $300,000 given now would have a tremendous financial and psychological impact on the campaign. He was nice, but he was adamant he would retain the stock until it reached a level he thought was worthy of contributing.

He was correct in that the stock continued to grow in value. It increased to $40 per share and I asked him to make the gift. Then $50 per share and I asked him to make the gift. Then $60 per share and I asked him to make the gift. Then $70 per share and I asked him to make the gift, noting how the gift was up to $700,000. That was more than double what he originally agreed to give but the same amount of stock and a real win-win situation.

His response was that the stock would go to $100 per share. I replied, "Great. Give now, and then when that happens, you can give more if you'd like." He refrained from giving, and we watched the stock go to $75 per share . . . and then it started to fall—$65, $58, $47, $33. Many times, I implored him to make the gift. He refused because "the stock would go back up." It fell to $30, $25, $18, $12. I watched helplessly as his original commitment could no longer be met, but still, $120,000 would be a very nice gift. His reply: "I can't give it now because it has fallen so much. When it bounces back, I'll give the gift." It didn't, and he didn't.

Isaiah 41:10

Do not fear, for I am with you; do not be afraid, for I am your God. I will strengthen you; I will help you; I will hold on to you with My righteous right hand.

While assisting another Christian school, I met a significantly wealthy couple who inherited land from a relative. The relative had been a major benefactor of the school. They indicated they had no use for the land, and since they had inherited it, they were interested in possibly making a gift to the school in honor of their deceased relative. With that in mind, I asked them to give the land to the school to sell, and the sales price would be credited as their gift to the campaign. However, rather than give the land, they determined they would tithe to the school based on the price they received from selling the land. There were offers for the land, but none ever came up to what the couple wanted. They held onto the land and watched the value of the land decrease as the real estate market declined. But, even then, particularly since the land was inherited, the reduced value would still have been a generous gift and a nice tax deduction for them. But instead, they took the property off the market.

I then suggested they use the land to establish a charitable trust to ensure a lifelong income for them based on the sale price after the land was placed in the trust. The school would receive the amount left in the trust after both were deceased. They chose not to do that because they said the value would increase and they wanted a lump sum payment when the land was sold.

The campaign ended and they never made a gift. The "better time to give" never came. So instead of reaping a nice tax benefit for themselves and a gift for the school by either selling the land or putting it in a trust, they retained a piece of property that continued to decrease in value.

1 Timothy 6:9
But those who want to be rich fall into temptation,
a trap, and many foolish and harmful desires, which
plunge people into ruin and destruction.

I was providing capital campaign counsel for a small Christian school. Historically, they never challenged their donors to give larger gifts. As a result, they always struggled financially. Because of the leadership's reluctance to meet with prospective major donors, I agreed to visit with some of the prospects to get the solicitation process started.

My first appointment was with a very successful business owner. I had previously conducted a feasibility survey interview with him in his mansion-like home. As I arrived for the appointment at his business office, I took note of the new Mercedes-Benz in his named parking place, the beautiful office building he owned, the spectacular decor of the office complex, and his dark paneled office with massive bookshelves and three large television screens showing the global financial markets. I was warmly greeted and ushered to a huge leather chair and provided coffee in a beautiful cup and saucer set.

He spoke enthusiastically of his ranch, horses, and his upcoming vacation. I updated him about the school and outlined the campaign. He listened intently. It was a fun time.

However, when I asked for a significant six-figure gift to be provided over a three-year period, his immediate reaction was, "Clark, you don't understand." (By the way, I get that a lot.) He went on, "I lost a million dollars in the stock market last year, but if things turn around, I might be able to do something next year." There were a couple seconds of silence, and then I asked him, "How much did you make in the stock market in the previous five years?"

He reacted by quickly leaning back in his chair with a "It's none of your business" look on his face. And, of course, it was none of my business. The reason for the question was to give him a different perspective to consider. His initial reaction turned to a blank stare. You could almost see the wheels turning in his head. Then he smiled and responded, "Five million." At that point I smiled and said, "So in the last five years, you've netted four million dollars in the stock market. Now let's talk about your gift." We did, and he did.

He "made" four million dollars in the stock market in five years, but like most of us, he looked at the immediate situation and, without realizing what he was doing, used that as an excuse not to give. With his situation in perspective—including noting that his investments in the stock market had no impact whatsoever on his house, car, business, vacations, or other possessions—he made a complete 180-degree turn and agreed to provide a sizable gift to the school.

Of course, most of us do not have the resources of this man. He oversees a larger portion of God's wealth in a year than many will oversee in a lifetime. My point is not about the wealthy but about how we consider giving in relation to our

DO WE CONSIDER GIVING IN RELATION TO OUR DAILY DESIRES THAT OFTEN RESULTS IN DELAYING OR NEVER FINDING THE TIME TO GIVE.

daily desires, which can often result in us delaying or never finding the time to give.

---

2 Corinthians 9:11–12

You will be enriched in every way for all generosity, which produces thanksgiving to God through us. For the ministry of this service is not only supplying the needs of the saints, but is also overflowing in many acts of thanksgiving to God.

Study Questions:

1. What is the reason, given in this chapter, for why Christians are not more generous? How does it relate to their perspective on giving?

2. How do people often use what-ifs and potential negative financial events as excuses for not giving, and what are the consequences of this mindset?

3. What is the story of the donor who agreed to give ten thousand shares of stock but continually delayed making the gift, and what does it illustrate about the dangers of waiting for the "right time" to give?

4. How did the wealthy business owner initially respond to the author's request for a significant gift, and what changed his perspective?

5. What does 1 Timothy 6:9 teach about the dangers of desiring wealth? How does it relate to the author's discussion of generosity and giving?

6. What is the significance of 2 Corinthians 9:11–12 in relation to the concept of generosity and giving? How can we apply this principle in our own lives?

7. How can we balance the need for financial prudence with the biblical call to generosity and giving? What are a few practical steps we can take to prioritize giving in our lives?

Action Points:

1. *Evaluate your own excuses for not giving.* Consider whether you have been using "what-ifs" or potential negative financial events as excuses for not giving.
2. *Take a step of faith in giving.* Consider taking a step of faith in giving, whether it's increasing your regular tithe or offering or making a special gift to a ministry or cause.
3. *Prioritize giving in your budget.* Consider prioritizing giving in your budget rather than viewing it as an afterthought or something to be done only when it's convenient. Ask God to help you develop a biblical perspective on giving and to prioritize it in your life.

8

No amount is too small

Oseola McCarty's life is a stewardship lesson for us all. She provided a $150,000 scholarship endowment for the University of Southern Mississippi to help pay tuition for students, preferably of African-American descent, who could not attend due to financial hardship. At first, I thought, *How nice for her to do that.* But then I read, as famed radio broadcaster Paul Harvey of years gone by used to say, "the rest of the story." It made me stop to consider my relationship with God and money.

Born in 1908, Oseola left school in the sixth grade, never to return, to care for her sickly aunt who needed home care. Later in life, having never married, she followed in the footsteps of her grandmother and became a washerwoman. For years she took in other people's dirty clothes to wash and press, often for less than a dollar a load. Those who knew her said, "She worked diligently, saved earnestly, and gave generously."

Needless to say, she lived a modest life—never owned a car, walked a mile to the grocery store, and didn't subscribe to a newspaper. She opened a savings account early in life and put aside funds for future needs. She was blessed that an uncle gave her the modest home she lived in from 1947 until her death in 1999. The small inheritances she received from the passing of her grandmother and mother went into the savings account.

Little by little, the account grew. A local attorney (for whom she did laundry) and a bank trust officer assisted her in estate planning. Upon her death, 60 percent of her estate ($150,000) was given to the university.[11] I am not saying everyone should live like Oseola McCarty, but can you imagine if all Christians embraced her pattern of saving and giving to be a blessing to others?

We convince ourselves to forgo the perceived small amounts for saving and giving because we think they cannot amount to much or accomplish much. How many wash loads did Miss McCarty have to do to establish an account that grew over time to provide a $150,000 gift? Oseola's accumulation of very small amounts eventually grew to help young people have opportunities not known to her.

How important is it for us to forgo some things so others might have opportunities in life beyond what their immediate personal circumstances will allow? How important is it to us to provide what could be the very thing a person needs to take the next step in achieving their life goal—or better yet, a relationship with Jesus Christ?

Mark 12:41–44

Sitting across from the temple treasury, He watched how the crowd dropped money into the treasury. Many rich people were putting in large sums. And a poor widow came and dropped in two tiny coins worth very little. Summoning His disciples, He said to them, "I assure you: This poor widow has put in more than all those giving to the temple treasury. For they gave out of their surplus, but she out of her poverty has put in everything she possessed—all she had to live on."

I have been blessed to provide counsel for scores of church capital campaigns. One item I always encourage to be included in the campaign is to have children from kindergarten through high school participate financially. Often, church leadership responds that it would not be worth the time and effort financially. Of course, the funds provided would not be enough to make a major difference in the campaign's financial goal. And, if you believe the campaign goal is only about money, then it would be correct to not engage the young people in the campaign.

There is an old fundraising saying: "People give to people for people." The need of a church campaign is not about a new building or an addition or increasing the staff or any other thing that requires money. The need of all Christian-related campaigns, church or otherwise, is to expand the kingdom by bringing people to a better understanding of their need to have Christ in their lives. Buildings, renovations, and added staff are the solutions by which the need to bring people to Christ is accomplished. To provide those solutions, funds are required.

Therefore, young people need to be involved in campaigns not for the small gifts they bring but to gain an understanding of the true purpose of a church. They need to understand that through their participation, they are assisting the congregation in reaching the goal of being a blessing to others.

It's not the amount of the gift but the understanding and sacrifice of the gift. When a teenager gives the funds from cutting grass or a first grader gives their father's spare change collected each night for a month (which could pay for a movie or a new toy), they learn a powerful lesson in sacrificial giving.

IT'S NOT THE AMOUNT OF THE GIFT, BUT THE UNDERSTANDING AND SACRIFICE OF THE GIFT.

Teaching biblical stewardship to young people will change their lives forever as they make decisions through the lens of being a steward of the Lord's wealth.

Matthew 19:14
Leave the children alone, and don't try to keep them
from coming to Me, because the kingdom of heaven is
made up of people like this.

I provided campaign counsel for a Christian school in a Southern state. The ongoing project is the construction of an entirely new campus, including buildings and athletic fields. It is a multi-million-dollar program. The facilities and fields are to be funded via major gifts and other financial relationships. However, a specifically stated goal of the campaign is to provide the furnishings for the preschool to twelfth grade via smaller gifts. These smaller gifts will combine to purchase chairs, desks, lab equipment, and smart boards. And these smaller campaign projects serve as an encouragement for those who can't provide large gifts to have meaningful participation in the campaign.

In structuring the campaign this way, it becomes meaningful to many more people. The joy of participation will be an encouragement to give again. As people realize their giving is important and is making a difference for the kingdom, they tend to increase the number of gifts even if they are never able to give a large gift.

Giving needs to be taught and patterned in a way that people begin to see that though their individual gifts may not be huge, their impact for the kingdom can indeed touch lives that need to hear the good news.

Acts 20:35

It is more blessed to give than to receive.

Study Questions:

1. What is the main lesson that Oseola McCarty's life teaches us about stewardship and giving? How can we apply this principle in our own lives?

2. How did Oseola McCarty's humble life and modest means not prevent her from making a significant impact through her giving, and what does this teach us about the value of small gifts?

3. What is the biblical principle illustrated in Mark 12:41–44? How does it relate to our attitudes toward giving and generosity?

4. Why is it important to involve young people in giving and generosity, and how can being involved shape their understanding of the purpose of the church and the kingdom of God?

5. What is the significance of Matthew 19:14 in relation to the importance of involving children in giving and generosity? How can we apply this principle in our own lives?

6. How can the structure of a fundraising campaign, such as the one described for the Christian school in a Southern state, encourage participation and giving from people of all ages and financial means?

7. What does Acts 20:35 teach about the value of giving? How can we prioritize giving in our own lives in order to experience the blessing of giving?

Action Points:

1. *Start small.* Consider starting a savings plan and giving regularly, even if it's only a small amount. Remember that small gifts will add up over time and make a significant impact.
2. *Involve the next generation.* If you have children or work with young people, consider teaching them about the importance of giving and generosity. Encourage them to participate in giving and generosity in a way that is meaningful and fun for them.
3. *Prioritize giving in your budget.* Consider prioritizing giving in your budget rather than viewing it as an afterthought or something to be done only when it's convenient.

9

Don't compare your giving with another's

Some years ago, a colleague of mine was meeting with the board of directors of an East Coast Christian school. They signed an agreement for counsel for a capital campaign. At this first meeting, the consultant reviewed the general outline of the campaign, including a campaign among the members of the board and their spouses.

At this point a member of the board interrupted the consultant to say the board would not be giving financially to the campaign. The reason given was that they put in a great deal of time working on behalf of the school and now others should step up to provide the needed funding.

The consultant explained the importance of the board's financial leadership to show they are not expecting others to do what they will not do. She explained that enthusiastic leadership is a key element of a campaign and gave examples of other campaigns that illustrated the value of board leadership.

The board spokesman remained adamant: "The board will not give financially to the campaign." At this point the consultant said, "Dickerson & Associates will not abide by that." She didn't make it back to her hotel before we were fired as the consulting firm.

Why would the board just assume others would provide the needed funding? Did they really think their modest giving to the annual fund and leadership of the school gave them a pass on giving to a campaign they voted to undertake?

The assumption others will give or should give all the funding to reach a goal really diminishes one's personal relationship with Christ—just like the servant in the story of the talents who buried the funds he should have invested on behalf of the master. The servant was rebuked by the master, and the funds given to him were taken from him and given to another.

The assumption "others should give" as an excuse for not giving illustrates a lack of appreciation for our blessings and displays ignorance regarding the sacrifice the Lord made on our behalf.

Often, I work with board members whose first reaction to a campaign goal is, "If we divide the number of prospective donors into the financial goal, that will give us the number everyone needs to give for the campaign goal to be reached."

Either they don't understand the concept of the individual stewardship relation with the Lord, or they just don't want to give any more. They feel if they match everyone else, then they are doing their part. Such Christians will not ask the Lord to guide them to the largest gift they could do. They give less because they believe matching what others give is all that is required.

Deuteronomy 15:10
Give to him, and don't have a stingy heart when you give, and because of this the LORD your God will bless you in all your work and in everything you do.

I heard a story about Ted Williams, the Hall of Fame left fielder of the Boston Red Sox. Many baseball experts have said that he had the greatest "hitting eye" there ever was or will be in the game. He is the last player to hit over .400 for a full season when, in 1941, he hit .406.

The story goes that, after he retired from active play, Williams was working with rookies during the Red Sox Spring Training. Williams watched intently as a young player time and again was having trouble picking up the curveball on its way from the pitcher to home plate.

Williams yelled to him, "Watch the stitches rotate on the ball."

As a former college baseball coach, I can tell you it is virtually impossible to watch the stitches rotate on a 95 mph fast ball. Such a pitch travels the sixty feet, six inches between the pitching mound and home plate in the time it takes to blink your eyes. That's not a lot of time to watch the stitches rotate on the ball. A curveball takes a bit more time to get to home plate, but not much.

Why, then, did Ted Williams tell the young man to watch the stitches? You see, Ted could see the stitches rotate on the ball. And, because he could, he assumed everyone should be able to as well.

In a similar vein many wealthy Christians who could give more assume others are giving at or near the same level. And they believe that if this is the case, there is no need for them to increase their giving.

Matthew 19:21–22
"If you want to be perfect," Jesus said to him, "go, sell
your belongings and give to the poor, and you will
have treasure in heaven. Then come, follow Me."
When the young man heard that command, he went
away grieving, because he had many possessions.

It's important to note that wealth is not the key factor in giving. Unfortunately, it is not unusual for people who are not of great wealth to think that if a rich person is giving to a ministry, then they do not have to give at all.

I know of a ministry in a relatively small Midwestern town. Word around town was that a very wealthy man, known of by almost everyone, was regularly giving large amounts of money to the ministry. It got to the point that people decreased giving to the ministry because they "knew" it was receiving so much from that one wealthy man. Of course, what they "knew" was not true. The wealthy man was giving, but the ministry was not at the top of his giving list.

In both the baseball and small-town examples, the point of generosity is missed. A wealthy person lacks generosity when they hold back because they think the others, who are giving less, will take up the slack. And those who can give, but to a lesser amount than a wealthy person, lack generosity because they think the wealthy person should give more.

The thing is, we are not to assume or even consider what others do. Paul taught the Galatians that "each person should examine his own work . . . not in respect to someone else. For each person will have to carry his own load" (6:4–5). So we should embrace the concept that giving is between us and our Savior on an individual basis. Do not compare yourself to others. Instead, take an introspective and prayerful approach of

> WE ARE NOT TO ASSUME OR EVEN CONSIDER WHAT OTHERS DO.

seeking what the Lord would have you give. And then give it, no matter what others are or aren't giving.

Matthew 6:3–4

But when you give to the poor, don't let your left hand know what your right hand is doing, so that your giving may be in secret. And your Father who sees in secret will reward you.

Study Questions:

1. What is the main point of the story about Ted Williams and the young baseball player, and how does it relate to the concept of giving and generosity?

2. What is the danger of assuming others will give enough? How can this assumption hinder our personal relationship with Christ?

3. What does Matthew 6:3–4 teach about the importance of giving in secret and not seeking recognition or reward from others?

4. What was the response of the board of directors of the Christian school when asked to give financially to the capital campaign, and what does this illustrate about the assumption that others will give?

5. What is the biblical principle illustrated in Deuteronomy 15:10? How can we apply this principle in our own giving and generosity?

6. How can the attitude that others should give all the funding to reach a goal diminish our personal relationship with Christ, and what is the biblical warning against this attitude?

7. What is the importance of seeking the Lord's guidance in our giving and generosity, and how can

we cultivate a heart of generosity and sacrifice in our own lives?

Action Points:

1. *Don't assume others will give.* Consider how you may be assuming others will give enough and how the assumption may be hindering your own giving and generosity. Ask God to guide you in your giving and to help you cultivate a heart of generosity.
2. *Give independently.* Pray for God's leading in your giving. Don't be concerned with what others are giving.
3. *Seek the Lord's guidance in your giving.* Consider seeking the Lord's guidance in your giving and generosity. Reflect on Deuteronomy 15:10 and ask God to bless you in all your work and in everything you do as you give generously and with a willing heart.

10

Reject the temptation (to be stingy)

Now, this chapter title may sound a bit harsh, but I believe it is something that needs to be addressed. This brings us full circle to the lady who turned her chair around. You see, it's important for us to understand that becoming a Christian does not automatically make someone generous. Martin Luther was quoted as saying, "The last thing to be baptized is someone's pocketbook."

Remember, 37 percent of people who attend church regularly never put anything in the offering plate. Never!

I know many Christians, of all socioeconomic levels, who are basically selfish. It's not a matter of not being taught about giving. They don't give because they don't want to give. They want to keep as much of what they have earned as possible. Their attitude is, "I've worked hard for my money, and I deserve to keep what's mine." They never seem to realize that the Lord blessed them with the talents to earn what they have so they can in turn bless others.

A colleague and I were consulting with a children's home. The board of directors unanimously voted to undertake a capital campaign. During the initial presentation, the board members were told that voting for the campaign meant contributing financially at some level to the campaign.

You can imagine our surprise when my colleague asked the chair of the board to make a three-year commitment of a certain level and was told, "No." When asked to make a lesser commitment, again the answer was, "No." When asked to make a one-time special gift, once again he heard, "No." Citing the need for 100 percent participation of the board, as was explained prior to the board of directors voting to move forward for the campaign, he was asked to give any amount of his choosing. Not only was the answer still "No," but he reported my colleague to the executive director for harassing him.

He was also furious when my colleague recommended he resign from the board if he would not financially support the campaign. I don't know about his giving to other causes, but to be the chair of the board, lead the vote for the campaign, and then give nothing is a bit much. For whatever reason, he simply did not want to give. And, of course, that is his stewardship decision to make.

My concern is when such people put on a good front to others, giving the impression of charitable giving and sacrifice, but knowing giving records are not publicly shared, never have any intention of giving.

1 John 3:17
If anyone has this world's goods and sees his brother in need but closes his eyes to his need—how can God's love reside in him?

Often, when speaking to people about providing a gift, they tell me, "Oh, you don't understand. I can't give. I'm on a fixed income." Several years ago, someone I knew quite well said to me, "Clark, you don't understand. I'm not able to give a gift. I don't get a paycheck anymore. I'm on a fixed income." I smiled and said, "Bob, how about this. I will live on your fixed income for the rest of my life, and you can live on my income the rest of your life. I'm not on a fixed income. Every check I get, I'll send it to you. Everything you get, you send it to me. Is that a deal?" Well, he frowned and became agitated. Eventually he told me he did not want to give.

You see, he was correct when he said he did not receive a paycheck anymore. His income came from dividends and other investments. He had an annual cash flow he called his fixed income—of a very significant six figure amount. It was not that he could not give. He just didn't want to give—and that is his decision to make. No one is required to give. But I'd much rather have someone tell me they don't want to give rather than make an untrue excuse.

There is a quote attributed to Mother Teresa, "If God's children suffer from hunger, homelessness, or abuse, it is not that God does not care, it is that his people have failed to act."

One of the questions I ask when conducting interviews for a confidential feasibility survey prior to a church campaign is, "Do you give 10 percent of your income to this church?" Most people answer "Yes." But I know many are not telling me the truth.

I know this because, prior to such a survey, I contact the local Chamber of Commerce to learn the average family income for the county in which the church is located. I multiply that figure by the number of families in the church and, while it's certainly not a perfect or exact method, it provides a good estimate of the collective family income for that congregation. Multiplying that figure by 10 percent, I determine an approximate amount of giving if all families in the congregation tithed. When that figure is compared to the annual offerings of the congregation, it is always a significantly higher figure. I have found time and again that if as many families tithed as said they did, the church would be running a large surplus or, better yet, would be able to fund more outreach ministries for the sake of Christ.

Let me hasten to add that the above story is not to say people are bad if they don't tithe—giving is a personal decision. I tell the story to raise this question: why do some people not tell the truth about giving?

I believe it is because they feel guilty. They know they could do more but choose not to give more. So, while the degree may vary, those who are not honest about tithing do so for the same reason as the fixed income person. They choose not to give or not to give more because they want to keep the money for themselves or spend it on something else.

This is their choice as a steward. They can spend God's money on anything they wish. It is not a question of salvation. It is a question of stewardship.

Some say, "You are not giving until it hurts." However, when I teach people how to solicit gifts, I tell them you want people to give until it feels good. People need to pray, "Lord, you know my family circumstances. You know my finances. You know everything about me—past, present, and future. Right now, I ask you to lead me in this decision of giving to this campaign (general fund, special project). Help me make a proper decision as a steward of your resources." I truly believe if we could teach people to simply approach

IT IS NOT A QUESTION OF SALVATION. IT IS A QUESTION OF STEWARDSHIP.

giving in that way, we could turn the world upside down for Jesus.

Psalm 25:4–5

Make Your ways known to me, LORD; teach me Your paths. Guide me in Your truth and teach me, for You are the God of my salvation; I wait for You all day long.

Study Questions:

1. What does Martin Luther's quote about baptism suggest about the relationship between Christianity and generosity, and how can we apply this principle to our own lives?

2. Why do many Christians choose not to give, despite being taught about the importance of generosity? What does this reveal about their priorities and values?

3. What is the biblical principle illustrated in 1 John 3:17, and how can we apply this principle in our own lives to demonstrate God's love to those in need?

4. What is the danger of making excuses for not giving? How can we cultivate a heart of generosity and willingness to give?

5. Why is it important to approach giving as a personal decision between oneself and God rather than comparing oneself to others or making excuses?

6. What does Psalm 25:4–5 teach about the importance of seeking God's guidance in our giving and decision-making? How can we apply this principle in our own lives?

7. How can we balance our desire to keep what we have earned with the biblical call to generosity and giving and what are some practical steps we can take to prioritize giving in our lives?

Action Points:

1. *Examine your motivations for giving.* Reflect on your own motivations for giving and consider whether you are giving out of a sense of obligation or a genuine desire to bless others.

2. *Approach giving as a personal decision.* Consider approaching giving as a personal decision between yourself and God, rather than comparing yourself to others or making excuses. Ask God to guide you in your giving and to help you make decisions that align with his will.

3. *Seek God's guidance in your giving.* Reflect on Psalm 25:4–5 and consider seeking God's guidance in your giving and decision-making. Ask God to make his ways known to you and to teach you his paths.

Final Thoughts

Years ago, I lived in Indianapolis. There is a mission for the homeless in the heart of the city. A family member who volunteered at the mission told me the following story.

The first time Joe, who most would call a bum, entered the mission, he was barely able to walk due to his drunken state. He was filthy, smelled to high heaven, and his clothes were torn and ill-fitting. To spend the night at the mission and, more importantly to Joe, to eat, it was mandated for every person to attend a chapel service conducted by a visiting local minister. As Joe attended chapel one night, God used the visiting minister to reach Joe and change his life forever. Joe accepted Christ, stopped drinking, reunited with his wife and family, cleaned up physically and mentally, got a job, and became a model citizen.

Joe never forgot the mission and the difference it made in his life. He volunteered on a regular basis to help those with whom he could relate. He mopped floors, helped feed people, cleaned up vomit, scrubbed toilets, and did whatever else was asked of him.

On another night another message was given by another visiting minister. At the end of the service, the visiting minister asked if anyone had anything to say. One man, bent over from a life of abusing his body, walked slowly to the front, kneeled on the concrete floor, and said, "I want to be like Joe."

The visiting minister did not know Joe and assumed the man had made a mistake. He said to him, "Don't you mean you want to be like Jesus?" To which the homeless man replied, "Is he like Joe?" You see, the man didn't know Jesus yet, but he saw Jesus through Joe, and, if Jesus was like Joe, then that was fine by him.

All Christians are like Joe in that we have received the very best gift possible—eternal salvation.

We do not live in a perfect world, but God has provided the solutions to our problems if we will only understand our role as stewards. The Lord is financially insolvent on this earth because he has given everything to his creation. It is up to his people to decide how to invest God's resources during the time on earth he gives them.

As our Leader and Provider, he has given each of us something that he expects us to use responsibly for his purposes. To some of us he has given more; to some of us he has given less. But his expectation of all of us is that we take his purposes seriously according to what we have. Let's share the time, talent, and treasure with which we have been blessed so that the blessings from God will be a blessing to others.

Romans 14:12
So then, each of us will give an account of himself
to God.

One of my favorite movies is *Saving Private Ryan*. The Ryan family lost three sons in battle during World War II. The War Department, as it was called then, made the decision to do all they could to keep the fourth son, who was on the European battlefield, from facing the same fate as his brothers. They did not want to send a fourth "I'm sorry to inform you" telegram to the mother.

HIS EXPECTATION FOR ALL OF US IS THAT WE TAKE HIS PURPOSES SERIOUSLY.

Therefore, a platoon, led by Captain Miller, was sent to find, and thus save, Private Ryan.

Along the way, several of the platoon were killed as they looked for the private. Eventually, they found him, but at the same time they were attacked by a German force wanting to capture the bridge Private Ryan's platoon was defending. More members of Captain Miller's platoon were killed. In the end, the bridge was saved, but Captain Miller was mortally wounded. With his last words he told Private Ryan, "Earn this, earn it."

Then the audience sees a close-up of Private Ryan's face some fifty years into the future. There stands Mr. Ryan, looking down at the gravestone of Captain Miller, as his wife and children watch from a distance. His wife approaches him and, turning to her, he says, "Tell me I've led a good life. Tell me I'm a good man."

Of course, I did not write the script nor direct the movie, and I don't know the point they wanted to get across at that moment. But to me, Mr. Ryan was trying to quantify his life—that in some small way, he had led a life worthy of the sacrifice Captain Miller and others made so he might live.

And, to me, that is the stewardship message. As Christians we know we can never repay the Lord for his sacrifice on the cross that led to his resurrection and the gift of eternal life for those who accept him as Savior. But, in some small way, by leading a Christian life and being a blessing to others through our time, talent, and, yes, treasure with which we have been blessed, we are saying "Thank you, Lord, for all you have done for me"

So, I ask, "Why aren't Christians more generous?" The answer to that challenging question is within each of us who, by faith, claim Christ as Lord. So many of us aren't more generous because we resist the call of God to be generous. And our lack of generosity means that fewer are hearing of the salvation that comes only through Christ.

Therefore, may it be that we turn our hearts toward God's message of stewardship and fully embrace his call to generous giving, so that we might be like our generous Father in heaven and be found fully faithful when Christ returns.

Action Points:

1. *Reflect on your role as a steward.* Consider how you can use your time, talent, and treasure to be a blessing to others. Ask God to guide you in understanding your role as a steward and to help you make decisions that align with his will.

2. *Seek to earn it.* Reflect on the sacrifice that Jesus made for you on the cross and consider how you can live a life that honors that sacrifice. Ask God to help you lead a life that is worthy of the sacrifice he made for you.

3. *Pray, act, serve, and give.* Consider the ways in which you can be a life-changing force for good in the world. Ask God to guide you in praying, acting, serving, and giving in ways that bring him glory and bless others.

Endnotes

1. "Church and Religious Charitable Giving Statistics," *Nonprofits Source*, nonprofitssource.com/online-giving-statistics/church-giving.

2. "Charitable Giving Statistics."

3. Denis Greene, "On Tithing: How Many Church Members Tithe," *Church Development*, April 3, 2019, church-development.com/what-percentage-of-church-members-tithe.

4. Jessica Eturralde, "Barna Report Newly Raises an Old Question: How Should We Tithe," *Religion Unplugged*, September 23, 2022, religionunplugged.com/news/2022/9/21/barna-report-newly-raises-an-old-question-how-should-we-tithe.

5. "Giving USA: U.S. Charitable Giving Totaled $557.16 Billion in 2023," *Indiana University Indianapolis*, June 25, 2024, philanthropy.indianapolis.iu.edu/news-events/news/_news/2024/giving-usa-us-charitable-giving-totaled-557.16-billion-in-2023.html.

6. "Church Giving Stats and Strategies for Adapting to New Trends," *Vanco*, vancopayments.com/egiving/asset-church-giving-statistics-tithing.

7. "Charitable Giving Statistics," *Nonprofits Source*, nonprofitssource.com, online giving statistics Church And Religious Giving Statistics 2024

8. Randy Alcorn, "How Pastors Can Model and Teach What God's Word Says About Financial Management," *Eternal Perspective Ministries*, January 17, 2018, epm.org/resources/2018/Jan/17/pastors-model-teach-stewardship.

9. Aaron Earls, "Protestant Church Closures Outpace Openings in U.S.," *Lifeway Research*, May 25, 2021, research.lifeway.com/2021/05/25/protestant-church-closures-outpace-openings-in-u-s/#:~:text=started%20in%202019.-,U.S.%20Protestant%20churches%20endured%20a%20difficult%202020%2C%20including%20starting%20the,from%20Nashville%2Dbased%20Lifeway%20Research.

10. "Bible Verses About Money and Stewardship," *Envoy Financial*, envoyfinancial.com/bible-verses-about-money-and-stewardship.

11. PKB INspire, "The Most Remarkable Woman You've Probably Never Heard of. The Incredible Story of Oseola McCarty," YouTube video, April 10, 2023, 7:48, youtu.be/vGFlNgQbyas?si=XiMV1LByP3hFHg48.

About the Author

Clark L. Dickerson, EdD

With forty-eight years of teaching stewardship and leading fundraising initiatives, including forty years as a fundraising consultant, Clark Dickerson has taught and consulted on development topics from capital campaigns to direct mail to board leadership.

Dr. Dickerson founded Dickerson & Associates in 1985 with a mission of assisting Christian organizations in reaching their mission and vision goals through the enhancement of their fundraising ministries. Dickerson & Associates grew to serve a nationwide clientele of hundreds of Christian schools, camps, colleges, churches, retirement communities, missions, and service organizations.

In 2012, Dickerson & Associates merged with another firm to form Dickerson, Bakker and Associates. Clark stepped down from all administrative responsibilities and continues to serve full-time as a fund development and stewardship consultant.

Clark has personally led over 250 capital campaigns and assisted scores of additional clients in other areas of fund development. He has spoken on fund development and stewardship at numerous Christian conferences and has written manuals on development topics. Additionally, Dr. Dickerson is a recipient of the Robert O. Fraley Award for a Lifetime of Innovative Development Service to Christian Development Officers.

Dr. Dickerson holds a BA in biology from Wabash College; a master's in education, with an emphasis in biology, from Indiana State University; and has a doctorate from Indiana University in higher education administration. He taught biology, was vice president of a college, and served with a mission organization in Eastern Europe prior to the fall of the Iron Curtain.

Clark lives in Montana with his wife, Sherry, and has three adult children, five grandchildren, and a dog named Ziggy.

You can contact Clark at:
P.O. Box 737
Gallatin Gateway, Montana 59730
Call or text: 303-886-4531

www.ingramcontent.com/pod-product-compliance
Lightning Source LLC
Chambersburg PA
CBHW051732040426
42447CB00008B/1099